Cogitation

Sam Love

Published by Unsolicited Press
www.unsolicitedpress.com

Copyright © 2017/2018 Sam Love
All photos Copyright© Sam Love
All Rights Reserved.

No part of this book may be reproduced or transmitted in any form or by any means without written permission from the publisher or author.

For information on ordering, contact publisher at info@unsolicitedpress.com

Unsolicited Press Books are distributed by Ingram.
Printed in the United States of America.

ISBN: 978-1-947021-12-9

Contents

Culture and Counter Culture	1
To Soar	2
The Perfect Holiday Meal	3
A Date With the Muse	4
Paper Oracle	5
Viva La Poetry	6
Black Lives Matter	7
Rainbow Soul	8
Hot Copy	10
The Real Subversives	11
Contrails	12
Crossing the Void	13
Be Careful With Your Wish	14
The Day Poetry Died	15
Arise	17
High Walls Make Good Neighbors	18
Serenity	19
Sitting Still	20
Defying Gravity	21
Mindfulness Incorporated	22
TAO	23
A Monastery Hires an Ad Agency	24
New Bern's Shrine	25
Photoshop for the Soul	26
Restoring Consciousness	27

Earth Consciousness	29
Viva La Tomato	30
Translucent Canaries	31
Pumpkin Odyssey	33
The Downstream Loop	34
Blueberry Mourning	35
Turtle Earth	36
The Last Laugh	37
Nature's Tiny Curse	38
Sayonara Humans	39
Hummingbird Laughter	40
Our Legacy	41
Life is Like a Roller Coaster	43
Yin Yang Love	44
Cell Phone Poets	45
Depression Memories	46
Harbinger of Spring	47
Lighting Up the Night	48
Lunacy	50
Main Street Porn	51
Mother's Thirty Seconds	52
RIP Bucket List	53
Seeking Out	54
Cultural Legacy	55
Rusted Dreams	56
Ghost Stumps	57
Rebels of the Universe	58

Yellow Jacket Proud	59
Velcro Dog	61
Burka Blues	62
Dogs for Peace	63
Highway Dreams	64
Big Blue Monster	65
Spring Hallucinations	66
House Hunting	67
Creative Camouflage	69
The Perfect Legacy	70
About Sam Love	71
Acknowledgements	72

Cogitate — verb: To think deeply about something; meditate or reflect.

In this over-stimulated fast-paced society you don't hear the word cogitate any more. We're so busy there is no time for it. Now only rebels and misfits cogitate. What a pity.

Culture and Counter Culture

To Soar

Celebrate a child's unbounded imagination
that attaches paper wings to a bicycle
and soars with birds above the earth
or transforms chairs and a blanket
into a castle safe from a hostile world

For a brief moment a child's world opens
unbounded by class, caste and privilege
so anyone can become a princess,
a president, or a rock star

Nurture this escape
before the so called real world
eats away at fantasy's edge
and reduces them to trolls
who imagine only the day to day

The Perfect Holiday Meal

Planning the meal required great care
until relatives created a cook's nightmare
RSVP's came back with emails to heed
every individual's unique dietary need

The vegetarians asked for no meat
so that spared a turkey the oven heat
We planned to toast with eggnog
Until the lactose intolerant
wanted no dairy based grog

So next we considered fresh fish
hoping it would make a pleasing main dish
A distant uncle worried about his ticker
became a real nuisance, that ol' stickler
I could hear the cook's bloodcurdling shriek
at the request of nothing with fins, face or beak

Then the exasperated cook let out a sigh
Saying at least there's fresh pumpkin pie
Until the next phone call added a request
Please nothing with sugar at my behest

That left only the homemade rolls
on a list that once resembled a scroll
Then a great aunt said prepare for me
a meal without wheat, a meal gluten free

Finally one day we gathered at the table
For the meal that's now a family fable
The chef did his best to please every critic
serving a single fruit salad, free of anything acidic

A Date With the Muse

To others it may look
like you're loafing
just shuffling through
but you've got a secret date
a date with the muse

It can happen any day
but the X on the calendar
often strikes in spring
as nature's reproductive juices
break their winter bond

Your eyes practically explode
after winter's gray pallet
surrenders to a landscape
splattered with bright colors

Your ears tune to a symphony
of avian melodies so loud
they are serenading
the most distant mates

Your body's nerves tingle
as you throw off winter's cloak
to expose naked skin
basking in sunlight's warmth

You pause by the river
and marvel at the ripples
as fish swim upstream
to their ancestral spawn

When your cell phone rings
and your boss asks if you're OK
just take a deep breath and say;
"I'm fine, it's just a poetry day."

Paper Oracle

The Appalachian calendar
hangs like a flat recycled altar
that my wife contemplates
for guidance every morning

While I contemplate my granola
she calls out, "The calendar says
today you should write a garden poem."
With my larder stocked with more garden poems
than canned vegetables
I'll ignore the calendar's guidance

Of course she's right
the calendar's daily wisdom
could change the world
 "Use a smaller plate"
"Live on less"
 "Slow down"
 "Celebrate the glory of the universe"
 "Choose the path of awe"

Who would have suspected
somewhere in the mountains
a reincarnated Buddha
sits on a rustic log cabin's swing
smiles a deep meditative smile
and rhythmically rocks back and forth

Viva La Poetry

Cultural darkness now
moves like a lunar eclipse
over the broken landscape

In obscure corners
of the digital realm
you can hear the primal screams
of poets shouting didactic rants
unshackled from opaque verbal puzzles
so loved by poetry professors

Fighting back requires
a clarity of language
to untangle the conscious
and unconscious knots
of racism, sexism, homophobia

Listen carefully to the embattled voices
of angry poets reconstituting
our shattered dreams

Black Lives Matter

Social crosshairs on police
street nerves ratcheted on edge
both sides living in fear
of a quick shot ending
the life they hold dear

On the street it's not like TV
where a doctor digs out the round
sews up the crimson wound
and the victim sticks around

Today's police are trained
to take perps down
with a center chest shot
from a high impact round

They'll load bullets like Golden Dot,
Golden Saber or Hydra Shock
Hollow rounds that mushroom out
guaranteeing wounds that bleed out

Fearing a slow brutal death
hunters consider inhumane
Hollow points are illegal
for deer, bear, or game

Hollow points are even
outlawed to fire in war
but they are sold all around
as a body stopping round

The streets may echo the chant
Hands up don't shoot
Black Lives Matter
But hollow points make it
Black Lives Splatter

Rainbow Soul

West Virginia 1988

Along the winding mountain road
brambles push through scattered rock
on a road that traces time backwards

To the hand laid rock foundation
with its cut stone chimney
poking above gnarled cherry limbs
piercing through wild vegetation

Today laughter no longer surfs the wind
and the chimney stands alone
in silent tribute to an unknown mason
whose calloused hands stacked the stones

What homophobic neighbor
would dare arson the erotic love
and front porch music that once
rolled down the mountain?

At the chimney's base
only fire hardened daffodils
are left to scatter their sun lit beauty
into the crannies of a charred dream

West Virginia 2017

For 13 dollars and 90 cents
UPS shipped the fired remains
of a gay soul whose life journeyed
through the cerebral and carnal
leaving smiles and pleasure in his wake

As we travelled to Appalachia
where he and his lover bought a house
that some Neanderthal arsoned to ashes
the skies drenched the path with tears

leaving me to wonder if his ashes
will trickle down the mountain
to nurture the rocky valley soil

As we gathered to celebrate
the showers moved on and the sky
cast down a splash of color
birthed by receding rain drops
refracting shimmering sunlight

We watched with reverence
as the rainbow painted a spiritual bridge
to welcome our friend home
so now he can savor the dance
of an afterlife with other
tortured souls that are finally free

Hot Copy

Poetry book blurbs are so boring.
In stark contrast romance writers
make their cover copy sizzle.
Consider how they might
describe my poetry.

Sam Love is an alpha male who loves
fishing, donuts, and obsessed heroes.
His poetry specializes in over-the-top,
sweet, and cheesy metaphors
that don't take all year to understand.
If you want something short and
sporting a hot cultural twist,
the Love man's poetry is for you!

His sweet as pie similes
will make "Fifty Shades of Grey"
seem like a children's primer.
They're as hot as the Texas heat
and they'll make sparks fly
like a red hot welding torch.

Blessed with the name Love
his sexy, and steamy lines will leave you
licking your lips for more hot poetry.
So just lay back with this brooding alpha hero
and savor his sweet rhythms
and enjoy the titillating spark
they ignite in your aging organs.

As you contemplate his metaphors
get ready for a roller coaster ride
because Love is one linguistically hot poet
ready to lasso your mind
and turn your world upside down.

The Real Subversives

I am grateful
to the rare individuals
who offered me keys
to unlock my small town mind

They worked selflessly
to expand my possibilities
beyond poverty, bigotry, darkness

I appreciate the librarians
who cultivate inspiration
that may one day blossom
into a doctor's new discovery
or a poet who crafts a phrase
that ignites a revolution

As rapid-fire media,
violent video games,
and saturation marketing
numb our culture
they cultivate an alternative world
of unbounded imagination

I celebrate the rebel librarians
who stand guard at the cultural barricades
promoting the joy of reading
in a twenty-first century world
threatened by forces extinguishing
enlightenment's flame

Contrails

As I scan the sky I wonder
what mysteries precede the ghostly contrails
Is the cargo hold filled with fruits and vegetables
commuting thousands of miles to a table?
Is there a casket returning from a war zone
Is a pet shivering in the aircraft's belly?

What secrets do passengers
dare not share with their seatmates?
Are they afraid the family reunion
will be an unmitigated disaster?
Are they fleeing an abusive relationship?
Do they worry Witness Protection
really didn't erase their past?

If the wispy white trails could
skywrite secrets on the blue palette
it would be more entertaining
than what now passes for television

Crossing the Void

On the Starship Enterprise
the void of space is the final frontier
but closer to planet Earth
the voids that divide us
present the real challenge

Peace and harmony require
crossing this chasm
to see the world through
the blinders on other's eyes

To look beyond the slogans
armored with glass ceilings,
racial bias, sexual harassment,
inequality and bloodied histories

With the planet's seven billion souls
longing for meaning and sustenance,
the voids between us are more dangerous
than the black holes of space

In this over crowded world
survival requires crossing the void
so pack your emotional baggage and
blast off across the unknown

Be Careful With Your Wish

With the winter weather warm and sunny
Tom found it tempting to skip yoga
to play another round of golf

As he sliced the little white ball
into the water trap
he joked he would ask
Santa for floating balls

To his surprise on Christmas morning
he awoke to a new sensation in his groin
Rolling over he recoiled in horror
at the site of two large bulges

Perhaps his wishes should be more precise
because Santa sometimes misunderstands
But always the optimist Tom realized
he would never need a life preserver

The Day Poetry Died

On November 8th America's poetry died
as the shock and awe of politics
left so many speechless
and closed the gates on
the shining city on the hill

As some mourned
the pent houses partied
leaving the media loud mouths
to puzzle how so many of Hillary's sisters
could fail to take a sledge hammer
to America's glass ceiling

When Trump primaried to victory
the Donald seemed the perfect foil
for a post feminist America
Certain that it was now her turn
the policy wonks filled her web site
with so many policy proposals
her positions became a blur
leaving her to admonish the pant suits
to be stronger together

Her cadre were confident few
would cast their vote
to Make America Great Again
with hate and venom spewing
into a media echo chamber
that promised the white race
a return to a mythical great country

Using Trump's own words
her campaign drew battle lines
around sexism and misogyny
Unfortunately their attack escaped
the hinterland's majority
who didn't know the meaning
of the Greek word for hatred of women

On election day no ancient Greeks
could mark their ballots
and Trump's rhythmic cadence
resonated with the masses
who watched him fly
his jumbo jet to victory

Arise

(inspired by the response to the inauguration)

Arise to the thunder of millions of hearts
beating with a resonance of freedom
lifting up fists of all ages
to the fiery sky, color shifting
from orange to an opalescent blue

Chanting messages so clear no one
could doubt the resolve
of a new dawn of compassion
flowing across the land

Young and old moving lock step
as millions lifted up signs
purified by dissent
awakening again the cry
Liberté, égalité, sororité

Three words to free the masses
held prisoner in a trance of digital illusions
Three words that will strike fear
into the hearts of tyrants
who suppress our better nature

Marching arm in arm
the legions echoed the rights
of all who dare champion
a future celebrating
the best of a civilization
founded on the blood of dreams

Draw strength from this tsunami
rolling across the land
like a wild unleashed spirit
awakening the masses
that dare to dream again

High Walls Make Good Neighbors

(with apologies to Robert Frost)

Something deep within
makes us love walls
reaching high enough
to bisect the sky

On one side
a false sense of security
On the other
an obstacle to overcome

After the construction
they require constant vigilance
for those tunneling under
and those climbing over

Continual patrols must search
for openings just large enough
to create an escape
from poverty's darkness

Openings illuminated
by a ray of light
that offers a glimpse
of prosperity's illusions

Before we build more walls
we should at least ask the question
Are we walling in or walling out?

Serenity

Sitting Still

Thousands of miles of travel
lead to a small village in India
where the guru instructs us
to learn to do nothing

Sitting still is harder than it looks
for an overloaded Western mind
that continuously dances
through time, and space

Defying Gravity

From Hatha to Happy Hour
the miracles of Spandex, Lycra and cotton
are ready to let your love shine through
and create the illusion of working out
without moving a muscle

The universal sound of "OM"
can tingle your inner thighs
and expand your mind, and body
with pants designed to tighten the sags
and flatter your silhouette

So comfy, soft, & sexy
there's a design for every taste
nondescript blacks and greys
for the muted look
skulls and peace symbols
for standing out while working out
tie dyes and camo patterns
for vanishing the dreaded butt dimple

Speed the transition from self-consciousness
to consciousness by diverting
wondering eyes away from your booty
with colorful downward arrows
creating the perfect skin tight detour

In this age of chasing more
yoga pants are the perfect fashion
for women to reveal
a little less of everything

Mindfulness Incorporated

Sitting quietly Buddhist monks
pursued mindfulness
by practicing peaceful contemplation
to empty their minds
and quiet the noise

As an antidote to our culture's
over stimulated meltdown
meditation is now fashionable
and the pursuit of mindfulness
has become a national past time

On the digital internet
products are cashing in
on the pop craze
of quieting the chatter
inside our heads

The ads in Mindful Magazine offer
an ap for one minute mindfulness,
Mindful Gray paint, Mindful Meats,
Mindful Tee Shirts, Mindful Tea
and Mindful Mayo

If you stress over mindfulness
you can sit on a Mindful Yoga mat
rub on some Mindful Body Lotion
and swipe on Mindful Deodorant
a salve that will elevate your armpits
to a new level of cosmic awareness

TAO

Like selecting three drops
of water from a flowing river
Buddhist monks select
just three from a sea of letters

A linguistic trilogy to describe
a universe in constant motion
like a flowing river
If the river stops
its identity changes
to become a pond

The Tao envisions a universe
in dynamic balance with a righteous path
yet as homo sapiens we perceive
space as mostly empty and cold
with the only psychic warmth
radiating from hope, love and empathy

If there is a master of the universe
perhaps it created us as an experiment
Odd little creatures left
to ponder if we are alone
and challenged to follow
the path of the Tao
to make the experiment a success

A Monastery Hires an Ad Agency

GOLDEN VOICED ANNOUNCER'S SCRIPT:
Has the modern world got you down?
Is earning a so-called living just too stressful?
Tired of chasing more material objects?
Ready to surrender in the war
to one up your neighbor?
Well, I've got an opportunity for you.
Our monks would love to have you
join them in chanting OM, Yes OM,
the universal sound encompassing all sounds.
A sound that's been around since
the creation of the universe.
This time-tested vibration is guaranteed
to lift you out of your material rut
into a state of heavenly bliss.
Monks are standing by
waiting for you to join them.
So start chanting OM today.
Who knows?
The universe may not be here tomorrow.

New Bern's Shrine

A splash of orange catches my eye
as a half dozen bald Buddhist monks
exit the historic district's sacred shrine
Pepsi Cola's drug store birthplace

Each of these purveyors of ancient wisdom
lovingly cradle a 16 oz. cup of Pepsi
With every sip of the addictive liquid
their lips curl into a satisfying smile

Taking a break from meditation
perhaps they even found a path
to enlightenment in the cola's old slogans
 "Pepsi--Exhilarating, Invigorating, and Aids Digestion"
Pepsi "more bounce from the ounce"
Pepsi "The soft drink leaves you brighter than it found you"

Still one has to wonder
if the vivacious ad models
offering a "Tempty and Tasty" break
tempted the celibate monks?

Photoshop for the Soul

Up pops a Facebook profile
with a lovely new photo
showing a friend's complete makeover
new hair color, new glasses
and an angelic smile

Air brushed blemish free skin
exudes a youthful countenance
only possible with the optical magic
wielded by a deft Photoshop hand

In her online neighborhood
this makeover signaled
a wonderful rebound
from her mapless detours
through the land of shadows

In her new Facebook fairy tale
happiness surrounds her
holiday meals are perfect
children are well dressed
and romantic love blossoms

Only those in the real world
could suspect how close
she danced to the edge
and still barely clings
to reality by a thread

These pixel touch ups
can improve the digital facade
but unfortunately
there's no Photoshop
for the beleaguered soul

Restoring Consciousness

Liberate your mind
Cut the cable
De-dish the dish
Celebrate the off switch
Restore pre-TV consciousness

Imagine a world where
producers don't addict us
twenty four hours a day
to blood, gore and sex

A world where children
aren't bombarded with
two hundred and fifty thousand
VIOLENT images before age 18

A world of natural stimulation
of chirping birds,
fire orange sunsets,
and star speckled night skies

Buddhists imagine the mind
a cage of chattering monkeys
where meditation can open
the creaky cage door
to let the monkeys escape

Meditation leaving the mind
so quiet the resonance
of past lives
will whisper in our ears

Earth Consciousness

Viva La Tomato

With hints of seasonal warmth
the tiny seeds break open
in the small peat pots
signaling the emerging spring

Soon the seedlings can be lovingly placed
into the garden soil nourished
with compost, crab shells
and rock phosphate

As the calendar pages turn
yellow blooms explode on green stems
until like magic the flowers
transform into miniature green tomatoes

When spring gives way to summer's heat
the fruitlings grow in diameter
until hints of red, yellow, orange
announce a culinary reward

When fully ripened
the sharp knife's first slice
creates an olfactory explosion
ready to titillate the tongue

The deep red slices stand
as a revolutionary counterpoint
to factory farmed imposters
oozing with impotent taste

Translucent Canaries

Around the rocky trail's bend
flashes of orange flicker
like Smokey mountain fire
as migrating Monarchs recharge
before taking flight to Mexico

So light and delicate
how could these orgasms of color
navigate thousands of miles
to their ancestral tree

Today fewer Monarchs migrate
as development and herbicides
decimate the milkweed
on which they lay their eggs
eggs that hatch into colorful caterpillars

Dressed in banded stripes the cats
gorge themselves on milkweed
and hang upside down on a stem
performing a rhythmic dance
of squeeze and pulsation
to disappear into a chrysalis cocoon
a safe incubator for a royal adult
with translucent wings

After summer cycles of life and death
only the fall hatch will fly
thousands of miles south
to astound natives who believe
the returning monarchs
are the souls of departed warriors

Now like a virtual canary
in nature's coal mine
fewer Monarchs overwinter
in the Mexican forest until
spring wakes the hibernators
and they take wing north

Pumpkin Odyssey

Pumpkin, pumpkin
orange and round
announces that fall
has come to town

A carved jack-o'-lantern
with glowing light
can make a scary face
for kids on Halloween night

The pumpkin symbolizes
Thanksgiving to a Pilgrim nation
and cooks make pumpkin pie
a culinary sensation

but in typical American style
chefs cooking for the holiday
get their pumpkin from a can
and throw the gourd away

Trash that creates municipal waste
wasting the water and chemicals
applied to the farmer's ground
that made it so plump and round

The Downstream Loop

Sparkling in the sunlight
the little plastic bag sails
from the mindless driver's hand
to drift among roadside weeds

No one bothers to retrieve it
and on county mowing day
whirring blades cut a grass swath
shredding the bag into gossamer slivers

The next thunderstruck downpour
carries the shreds through the watershed
to the larger boiling stream
to the tidal marsh
to the Atlantic ocean

The Gulf Stream's sun and waves
pulverize the slivers into tiny bits
creating a perfect culinary delicacy
for large schools of filter feeders
Small fish that mistake plastic globules
for aquatic eggs and plankton

Larger fish like Sea Trout and Tuna
cut a swath through the schools
and devour the tiny fish, concentrating
the petrochemicals up the food chain

For dinner we purchase the wild-caught Tuna,
let the fish monger filet the toxin-laden flesh,
pack it in ice, and store it in a virgin plastic bag
A bag that completes the ecological cycle

Blueberry Mourning

It's a January frost-free miracle
in my North Carolina supermarket
It's a two-for-one blueberry sale
so I add them to my shopping cart

Secure from the freaky outside cold
the Chilean bleuets look perfectly cozy
in their crystal clear plastic containers
They look so comfy, I wonder if they
still dream of summer in South America

As I eat my morning oatmeal
I ponder the adventure stories
of this well-travelled fruit
Could it tell me about the toxic sprays
that made it picture perfect?
Was it picked by a shaker machine
or by campesinos breaking their backs?

How was its 4,136-mile plane trip
from the Chilean farm to Florida?
Did it enjoy its 869-mile
truck trip up the interstate?
How many miles per gallon
does a Chilean blueberry get?

Some time this summer
local pick-your-own blueberries
will ripen on nearby vines
and they can take a short cut
across the river to my morning bowl

Then breakfast will be more enjoyable
when my mind doesn't have to digest
so many perplexing questions

Turtle Earth

The Lenape creation story-- Nanapush asks
who will let me put the cedar branches on top of you
so that all the animals can live on you?
And the turtle said, "you can put them on me
and I'll float on the water."

In a vision the Native American holy man
sees the animals bringing earth from
under the water to make land
on the back of the turtle
creating a continent, a verdant Eden
where plants and animals flourish

In another dream the Indian shaman
sleeps a long sleep and awakens
to see a barren steampunk turtle
filled with writhing serpents
thrashing their rattler tails through portals
in the armor plated earth's shell

This hollow eerie sound
resonates with a dry rattle
of primordial notes memorializing
the emerging death of nature

The Last Laugh

Imagine the sex life of bacteria
No cumbersome courting for a mate
just every ten minutes they can split
their single cell into two,
then two will split into four

As masters of rapid adaptation
they can flourish in hellish places
acidic hot springs, barren soil, brackish water,
radioactive waste and the human gut

In our body we have ten times
more bacteria than cells
Probiotics are the good ones
and germs are the bad ones

Plain soap could do the job
but instead we use antibacterials
to cleanse counters, sterilize food
and sanitize the baby's butt

Antibacterials only kill 99 percent
so you have to wonder about the one percent
Are they planning a counter attack
with super resistant germs

If they could do a belly laugh
they'd be doubling over
because the real joke is on us
humans who think we rule the earth

Nature's Tiny Curse

Mother Nature can be a bitch
As our exhausts trigger wilder weather
she amps up her springtime curse

of tiny odd shaped sperm
freed from tree, weed and flower stamens
to fill spring wind currents
with males searching
for a chance mating
with a female pistil

Unfortunately for us
the male gametes
create allergies
as they mistake the human nose
for a plant's female organs

Sayonara Humans

To make a dab of honey
I have to sample nectar
from one hundred flowers
A pound could require visits
to two million flowers

Now our colonies are collapsing
Pesticides, parasites
and climate change
are killing us off
and you'll miss us
when we're gone

We pollinate one third of your food
so if you like your fruits, vegetables,
almonds, apples, strawberries,
blueberries, potatoes, peppers and pears
get ready to kiss them good bye

Sayonara humans
eating just corn and soybeans
is going to get really boring

Hummingbird Laughter

The oily seeds in my backyard feeder
create a regular dinner party
with black sheened Grackles swooping in first
sloppy, aggressive diners
knocking morsels to the ground
to a lower caste of brown suited Doves
scavenging downstairs for left overs

With the dinner party in full blast
the fire red Cardinal
flies in like a Kung Fu fighter
to scatter the large black bullies
and gorge himself at the feeder
Patiently his less colorful mate waits
her turn to savor sunflower seeds

After they dine, the Kung Fu Cardinals
clear an opening for more delicate guests
common Sparrows, the Towhee
and the belle of the ball, the House Finch
dressed in bright colorful plumage.
A bird escapee from wire framed cells
to mate with others in the wild

Nearby at the liquid feeder
a Hummingbird hovers,
laughing at the seed eaters
whose clumsy beaks can't savor
the bliss of sweet flower nectars.
Laughing at evolution that freed it
as a competitor for top bird

Our Legacy

As obsolescence
rules the market
permanence becomes
a museum exhibit

Native American potters
must be smiling
knowing their earthen art
will outlast our digital legacy

Still our legacy will be secure
in mounds of disposables
no one can repair
and nature cannot degrade

Life is Like a Roller Coaster

Yin Yang Love

I chuckle at TV's singles ads
offering to search their database
for a mate with my same interests

A computer match program
would never put us together
We are so different, you and I

You accept God
I struggle with the big question
You love meticulous order
I find creativity in chaos

You love people in books
I love people at parties
You balance your checkbook
I hope the bank gets it right

Only the Eastern Yin Yang concept
can explain our thirty years together
Yin Yang, an ancient Chinese symbol
of black and white opposites
intertwining to create a unity

Computers could never calculate
a whole from universal opposites;
light and dark, hot and cold, fire and water,
masculine and feminine, life and death

That's why you'll never see a dating ad
featuring opposite magnetic poles
rushing toward each other
to mate like lustful lovers

Still the real mystery for me
is how you decided
to take a chance on us

Cell Phone Poets

At the open mike
I watch younger poets
thumbing their "I" gadgets
to read their poetry

When I read my poetry
I'm sure they think
there's the old fart
shuffling his printed pages
sharing his angst
at what we call culture

But I have a secret
for the cell phone poets
who electronically store
their broadsides
about lust, unrequited love
and adult insanity

Bugs, malware and
cloud outages will vaporize
their digital poetry
long before archaeologists
uncover my printed poems

Depression Memories

Growing up I remember our empty log smokehouse
where hams once dangled from darkened rafters
A ramshackle building that leaned to one side
a decaying monument to a past I never knew

Still standing it stood empty as a ghostly reminder
of wounds left by the Great Depression
a darkened period that altered our life
and forced a frugality slow to heal

In spring these haunting memories
still emerged as we planted a garden
to yield arrow straight rows
of sweet corn, butter beans,
heirloom tomatoes, turnip greens
and blood red strawberries

In fall this garden succumbs to canning
to fill the pantry with crystal jars
all lined up as Depression memories
in case another economic abyss
clinches the family's belt

Harbinger of Spring

On a freaky February day
a mutant daffodil burst forth
in a radiant bloom
ahead of crocuses, snow drops,
pussy willows and anemones
It's stalk stretches skyward
to test if it is now spring

A late frost soon shatters
illusions of its sun-yellow bloom
and warns its relatives
to lay dormant
until the thermometer
levitates above the frost line

Lighting Up the Night

Two great American icons
the automobile and Hollywood
birthed drive in theaters
tall edifices that stood
like a thick blade slicing the sky

Here shiny post war cars
lined up like a formation of soldiers
to salute the declining daylight
On the driver's side window
grey metal die cast speakers
filled the car with low fi sound

At the outdoor drive in
features like "Grease" gave way
to cheap horror flicks that assaulted
the screen with gory scenes crafted
to motivate the most reluctant dates
to slide closer on the 1950's bench seats

Today only a few outdoor theaters
survive the real estate explosion
of suburban malls and apartments
On the remaining drive in screens
projectors still bathe the screen
in a Xenon glow of second run movies

If the screens could talk
they would tell stories
of children sleeping in the back seat
of heavy petting that got out of hand
of charred hot dogs grilled in the back lot
and local bands playing
to celebrate the setting sun

In the late twentieth century
HBO, DVD's and Netflix
closed the final chapter
on most out door drive ins
The screens faded to white
to never again light up the night sky
with tales of romance and horror

Lunacy

Poor Luna, the Roman goddess
who gives birth to the new moon
the guardian of the feminine realm
of monthly cycles, and fertility

In the guise of this slivered moon
she is the Maiden Goddess
so fresh and virginal
a harbinger of a new beginning

Then as her fullness increases
she becomes the Mother Goddess
pregnant with an abundant life
and infinite possibilities

After her light's fullness wanes
she is celebrated as a crone
an ancient guardian of magical arts
and a source of wiccan power

In this dimming of nocturnal light
humans fear the soul's lunacy
where werewolves and wombats
roam the eerie nightscape

Finally a new moon
heralds the rebirth of a cycle
and overcomes irrational fears
to celebrate new beginnings

Main Street Porn

If a media "it" girl
needs a virile video
they can enlist the services
of a wardrobe malfunction specialist

As Janice Jackson's flash of a side boob
morphed into the sheer vagina dress,
today's publicity requires
an even more risqué look

If you don't want to totally "freeboob" it,
you can opt for nipple covers
like Commando's Stick-on Low Beams
or Bristols' Adhesive Nippies,
that blend in with the ultra edge

Keep your girls from popping out
with Victoria Secret's Double-Sided Stylist Tape
One side sticks to the fabric
and the other to your skin
securing everything in place

Avoid a tabloid supermarket cover
showing too much of your nether region,
with the Camelflage Lace Thong,
available in multiple skin colors

But if you really want to go all the way
go for the full commando look
with Nordstrom's Commando Cotton Thong
coupled with Breast Petal nipple covers
guaranteed to avoid an unwanted slip

After selecting the ideal designer combo
switch on your iPhone flash and snap a picture
because the sheer dress might look perfectly tasteful
in the boutique mirror, but a piercing flash
could be a whole other scene

Mother's Thirty Seconds

For a fleeting broadcast moment
my elegant mother smiled down
from the Jumbotron in Times Square
as a teaser for NBC's nightly news

How ironic her art or community service
never made national headlines
but her recognition of a long dead sister
in a yellowed Alabama photograph
led a TV story about a professor's research
on pictures as memory triggers

How odd that someone
could be on national television
for only remembering fragments
of the hidden childhood memories
that Alzheimer's forgot to destroy

Andy Warhol said in the future
we all get 15 minutes of fame
mother got thirty seconds

RIP Bucket List

Like a ghost my bucket list
of dream items haunts
my final count down

Once I laid out some rich fantasies
A grand cross country RV trip
A coast-to-coast poetry reading
Fly fishing in an Alaskan stream
Restoring a Studebaker Golden Hawk

At first my bucket list
just sprang a small leak
as my real estate nest egg cracked
like Humpty Dumpty's autopsy

Then the diminished dreams
turned into a steady stream
as the stock market
started down and
medical costs started up

But maybe the bucket list
didn't really matter because
travel is a pain in the butt with:
traffic snarls, high gas prices
and cracks in my back that sound
like Fourth of July fireworks

So I'll just put the bucket list
out of sight and out of mind
and move it to a safe place
with a plan to recover it
when I win the lottery

Seeking Out

My maleness roams the Internet
seeking a home for my poetic diatribes
Clearly I'd have more options
if I fit into a more hip category

Hashtag Queer only seeks work
from queer-identified writers
Upper Rubber Boot limits its call
to those who identify as female,
non-binary, or a marginalized sex

Others only want pieces from
gender-nonconforming
or non-heteronormative writers
I can't even imagine the slush pile
soliciting love poems from asexuals

After multiple searches
I've found my niche
Oregon now accepts non-binary
so I am one-half of the binary category
ensconced in an evolving tri sexual world

Cultural Legacy

Rusted Dreams
(on visiting an antique automobile junkyard)

The material world offers
a plethora of automotive models
V8's to enhance the ego
Leather seats to sooth the soul
Convertibles to ameliorate sadness

These sparkling new objects
become shimmering mirrors
that reflect a false happiness
for lost consumer souls

In time the mirror becomes cloudy
and rust corrodes our shiny dreams
unleashing nature's antidote to optimism

Ghost Stumps

White laminate counters, dirty and cracking
look like an obscenity of 1980's chemistry
Once the pinnacle of kitchen style,
they now look alien
in a Southern Victorian lady,
crying out for restoration

The old house's Heart Pine bones
still stand strong as a tribute
to over 100,000 square miles
of ancient Atlantic forests
with trees that reached hundreds
of feet into the southern sky

Centuries of slow growth
produced a steel hard wood
impervious to mold, insects and rot,
but vulnerable to steam powered
razor sharp steel blades

Natives respected the forest that
sustained them, but the whites
saw product yielding obscene profits
from iron hard lumber to build
wharves, mills, homes

In mere decades the ancient giants vanished
from the South's coastal forests
leaving only ghost stumps
watched over by faster growing soft pine

Now the old mills constructed of Heart Pine
sit silent waiting for salvagers to strip
the hollow factories of "antique" boards
hard enough to create a kitchen counter
for my restored Victorian

Rebels of the Universe

Our universe is so cold and dark
just a vast stark emptiness
punctuated with flashes
of explosive celestial light

In all this vastness
we are the rebels
the odd organic creatures
gifted with the spirit of love,
compassion and hope

Just odd rebellious
small bipedal creatures
left to ponder our fate
and wonder if we are alone

Yellow Jacket Proud

In 1965
gasoline costs
35 cents a gallon
a new Mustang sports car
2,400 dollars
a new house
13,000 dollars

In 1965
male hormones raged
as mini skirts rose to new heights
topped by towering bouffant hair

In 1965 45 rpm big hole records
sounded the Beatles call for Help
and the Beach Boys seduced us
with California sun and surf

In 1965
Vietnam seemed far away
from a sleepy Alabama town
where parents left the house
for real jobs in local factories
and on weekends our old cars
could cruise the Dairy Dream
A hangout that served
Alabama health food
french fries, cokes and hamburgers
all washed down with splashes
of black market bourbon

Looking back Aliceville seemed
like a Norman Rockwell town
where doctors made house calls
the Palace Theater featured Saturday matinees
and boys could skinny dip
with no concern for fashion
Until prom night when we

dressed in sports coats, white shirts and ties
to escort our dates in colorful dresses
that overflowed car seats

Aliceville's Main Street shut down
for the homecoming parade
where the team mascot a Yellow Jacket
crafted of crepe paper and chicken wire
could sting rival York's Jaguars

Looking back 1965 high school
seemed like a golden era
of youthful optimism for graduates
where tomorrow would be
ours for the taking

Then the music got louder
the draft gambled with our future
marijuana muddled our thinking
busing ripped apart neighborhoods
and factories started closing

But for those of us who grew up
in this once-upon-a-time Alabama town
high school strengthened us
to take life's punches
and stand up Yellow Jacket proud

Velcro Dog

With great literary flourish
the ads for rescue dogs
help abandoned, lonely pets
find a human forever home
as if any of us lives forever

Redford, a mixed something
or other, becomes a big handsome boy
who is the perfect mate for Sasha,
an elegant lady with a gentle personality

Clarence, the velcro dog,
will stick to your side
and Rusty, the stray, could
become your forever friend
and follow you anywhere

Human eligibles on computer dating sites
could learn a lot from the dog ads
where a chunky girl with a soft coat
is transformed into a snuggle companion
who isn't very demanding

And an aging male becomes
the pick of the pack who is over
his puppy stuff and ready
to crawl under the covers
on days he is up for it

Note: Every descriptive phrase in this poem came from an actual dog rescue ad.

Burka Blues

You have to wonder
what's happening as eyes peer
through Burka slits
to watch Western women
shoulder automatic weapons
and hot rod armored vehicles

The Quran instructs men that "good women are
therefore obedient, guarding the unseen as Allah
has guarded; and those on whose part
you fear desertion, admonish them,
leave them alone in the sleeping-places and beat them"

Long after our troops have withdrawn
images of Western warrior women
will smolder behind the Burkas,
making male egos tremble
at the cultural revolution
about to shatter their isolated world

To speed the revolution our drones
should start book bombing
walled courtyards with Arabic translations
of feminist literature
 "The Feminine Mystique," "The Second Sex,"
"The Vagina Monologues" and "The Female Eunuch."

Because so many Muslim women
were never allowed in schools
illiterate eyes will fall on some pages
but enough will catch the feminist spirit
to stir a cultural revolution
that will shake Muhammad's grave

Dogs for Peace

Pity the poor peace symbol
Once we hand drew them on signs
to march and let the world know
we should give peace a chance

A graphic, so simple, so elegant
Just a circle and three lines
calling for a revolution
to give peace a chance

Today Wal-Mart's website
is your peace symbol headquarters
Just type peace symbol in its search box
and you can order it on military style hats,
trash cans, underwear, bed spreads, jewelry
and much much more.

Wouldn't your cat or dog
love the peace symbol
on "a funky tie dye ID,
the perfect groovy accessory
for any pet still spinning the Grateful Dead
and daydreaming of Woodstock."

What incredible irony
in a world overflowing
with war and hatred
peace has gone to the dogs

Highway Dreams

Parallel to the manicured four lane
a narrow two lane road
snakes past gravel entrances
to broken dreams

Rusted gas pumps sit idle
with mechanical numbers frozen
in a time when a gallon of regular
sold for ninety nine cents

Rickety wooden stands
for fresh-picked fruits and vegetables
sit empty, abandoned by farmers
bankrupted by Wal-Mart's foreign produce

Faded hand-painted signs
announce antiques and mountain curios
once lovingly crafted by locals
who never called themselves artisans

A neon filled electric sign
will never again blink on
announcing the café is open
with hot coffee and fresh-baked pies

These buildings with peeling paint,
rotting wood, and broken windows
stand as historical monuments
to a local person's broken dreams

An independent country dream
of owning your own business
before the interstate stole customers
now flying past at seventy miles an hour

Big Blue Monster

Early one winter morning
the future comes rumbling
down the side of my street
in the guise of a garbage truck

Pausing by the curb
the truck's only occupant
extends a giant mechanical claw
to the waiting tall green can

It's robotic fingers straighten
and fondle the plastic container
with vice-grip delicacy
before flipping it into the air

At its zenith the lid flops open
to dump a week's assemblage
of plastic wrappers, tissues,
food waste, and assorted trash

Once upon a time one driver steered
and two workers hung off the back
where with the agility of circus performers
they wrestled the large refuse bins

A nimble finger would press a button
to compact the trash into a sculpture
of found art to be displayed only briefly
at the county's overflowing land fill

So the next time you hear politicians
talk job creation, think about the ghosts
in bright orange jump suits
who once hung off the truck's back
until the robot claw underbid them
and put their families on food stamps

Spring Hallucinations

Oh the joys of an old house
with drafts that chill your bones
refrigerate your bare head
and lull your brain into standby

Winter winds whistle through
every tiny opening
around windows, doors
outlets, floor boards

The ancient heating unit
labors to fight the draft
by cranking out so many BTU's
global warming becomes a great idea

Outside the snowy cold is so brutal
any thought of winter romance
freezes under layered blankets
leaving hallucinations of a spring thaw

House Hunting

Some people hunt for houses
and some houses hunt for people
I discovered this the hard way
as I monitored an internet house sale

With the on screen clock ticking down
no one bid in digital time and space
Until, in the last nail biting moment,
two of us duked it out
in hundred dollar increments.

Gritting my teeth, I placed a final bid
as my bank account flowed red ink
Holding my breath the screen
finally clicked to zero

And the prize --A 110-year-old house
with a leaking roof, rotting wood,
peeling paint and openings
for squirrel condos

I knew it cried out for saving,
but I didn't know that once
a secret coven of wiccans
gathered regularly on the third floor

Some nights I imagine I hear the group
circling the pentagram painted
on the splintered attic floor
chanting to spirits of water, earth, and fire

The next owner had no appreciation
of spiritual art and smothered
the five pointed star with latex paint

Little did I know the pentagram's spirit
would ooze through the paint,
and surf the digital realm until
it found me, its architectural savior

Clearly, real estate ads
never tell the whole story

Creative Camouflage

As a master of creative camouflage
I assume the disguise
of an old white guy

No florescent body tattoos
because my mind is tattooed
with images from so many
past psychic journeys
I've already got my passport to Mars

No weird long purple hair
or giant discs wedged into my ear lobes
to make me look like a Maasai warrior
shaking my spear and shield
in the our raging culture wars

Being disguised as a normal
I can slip among the blissful unnoticed
and hijack their observations
without them ever suspecting
an alien escaped from the creative class
to chronicle their march to the cliff

The Perfect Legacy

Celebrate your new home
by planting a tree
transplanting a shoot
or burying a tiny acorn

In time a strong limb
will be there when children
need to soar on a swing

As the trunk reaches up
limbs will block the sun's heat
until fall when the colored leaves
can nourish rich brown compost

Other homes will appear as birds
build nests in cloistered limbs
and squirrels weave a winter nest

After you are gone the majestic tree
could be your natural legacy
as neighbors and family celebrate
the one who sewed the seed
and nurtured the sprout

About Sam Love

Sam Love is an award-winning writer living in New Bern, NC. He has published numerous nonfiction articles in magazines that include *Smithsonian*, and *Washingtonian*. In addition to another poetry book, he has two published novels, *Snap Factor*, and *Electric Honey*. His poetry has been published in numerous journals.

Acknowledgements
These poems have been published in the following publications:

Velcro Dog	*Kakalak*
The Perfect Holiday Meal	*The Lyricist*
The Downstream Loop	*Duke University's Eno Magazine*
Blueberry Mourning	*Duke University's Eno Magazine*
Turtle Earth	*Duke University's Eno Magazine*
Viva La Tomato	*Duke University's Eno Magazine*
Depression Memories	*Voices on the Wind*
Spring Hallucination	*Voices on the Wind*
Defying Gravity	*Flying South*
Mindfulness Incorporated	*Flying South*
To Soar	*Poetry in Plain Sight (storefront poster Winston Salem)*

www.ingramcontent.com/pod-product-compliance
Lightning Source LLC
Chambersburg PA
CBHW021449080526
44588CB00009B/759